T0095028

becki justbecki

A Glimpse inside My Bag of Abuse

REBECCA HENDERSON

iUniverse, Inc.
Bloomington

becki justbecki
A Glimpse inside My Bag of Abuse

iUniverse books may be ordered through booksellers or by contacting:

iUniverse
1663 Liberty Drive
Bloomington, IN 47403
www.iuniverse.com
1-800-Authors (1-800-288-4677)

ISBN: 978-1-4759-3011-5 (sc)
ISBN: 978-1-4759-3009-2 (e)

Library of Congress Control Number: 2012909624

Printed in the United States of America

iUniverse rev. date: 5/30/2012

Contents

Hidden

Sometimes I feel like a ghost roaming around in the darkness
hidden from all eyes, even my own.
No one can see this darkness that treads over me, this burning
   in my chest,
this longing in my heart for the light that has yet eluded me.
Theresa Amato
Written by a budding poet.

Acknowledgments

I want to acknowledge the following individuals and groups, without which this book would not have been possible:

My husband & family
My dog Dot
CalCopa Massage School
Braille Institute
Guide Dogs for the Blind
Gold Rush Guides
My screwed-up parents
My editor's
and Lara R, Thank you with all my heart!

NOTE: To protect myself and my family, I have made subtle changes to some settings, names, or places.

Introduction

In each chapter of this book I bring a glimpse into the world of abuse and survival. I share my life experiences openly and freely. I will share my reflections and how those events shaped my life today.

Everyone needs and deserves to feel valued and special to someone.

There will be some who recognize my journey to fill the void. Very few women survive abuse, and even fewer women survive and feel comfortable in their own skin. My early life was a turbulent world filled with chaos, beatings, and mental illness. Alcohol abuse, kidnapping, and murder were components of my adult life.

I never gave up. Through it all, I never quit. In telling my story, I let my sick sense of humor and perspective come through even while discussing mental illness, incest, and what I ate for dinner—that means inserting my personality into my writing. This is my story—my voice.

I was completely unaware that I should be asking myself questions like this: *Why do I keep making bad choices? Why do bad things keep happening to me? Why?, Why?*

It has taken me years of hard work and much self-reflection to come to where I am today. I made a journey to find out why I am the way I am. This is my message: Listen to your intuition. Take chances. You may find strength and inspiration in my story.

becki justbecki

I recognize that many people feel internal shame. The population, for the most part, does not identify shame as shame. Shame takes your self-esteem and devours it. It ends relationships. Internal shame can cause eating disorders and other forms of self-abuse.

I kept self-abusing long after leaving a toxic environment. Steps can be taken to release the feeling of shame and the effects these feelings create. Shame will erode relationships. You can't shower it off. You can't outrun it. No matter what I did, shame influenced everything. That is what I felt at points in my life, and I had to climb out of the abuse.

Now when I come across people in an emotional hole, I throw in a rope, but it is up to the person in trouble to grab it. Throwing a rope could mean something so simple as giving an item of value or a simple card explaining why that person is special to you.

Recently, I met a woman who was in massage school, and she had had some hard emotional times. I don't know what it was, but I felt her pain. It was her birthday, and she had no family around. I went home and dug through my things and found the perfect gift: an opal necklace from my collection. I gave her the tiny box.

She was so moved that someone she barely knew cared that it was her birthday. She started to cry. I did not know what to do so I excused myself and went home. On my walk home I thought about what had just happened, and it felt so wonderful to let someone know she was special.

Every person deserves to feel that he or she matters. I also think everyone deserves to feel that inner joy from giving to others. I'm not talking about donating or giving money to the person on the corner with the "give me" sign. I'm talking about random acts of kindness.

For example, on the television show *The Osbournes,* Sharon Osbourne had colon cancer. Some media outlet had shown the gates to their home, and there was a demon or gargoyle-style head on the big gates. I found a pin in my collection from the 1800s that was the same gargoyle demon head. I looked up her address and wrapped up the pin and put a little card with it.

My husband and I drove to the Osbournes' to deliver the gift to her. That was so cool. About a month later I got a note and a photo from her thanking me for the gift and saying that she was doing better.

For this book I chose the title *A Glimpse inside My Bag of Abuse* because everyone has baggage. Everyone! I decided to share a glimpse of mine with you. There is a possibility to bring hope to some and humor to others. Energy does not dissipate; it moves on and on. This is a way for me to share some experience, wisdom, and energy.

I stood on my own. I promised myself I would do everything in my power to make my way. I feel that I can share my experiences to help others find out how to make positive change. I have learned how to deal with pain. That does not mean that I did not feel pain. I have taken responsibility for everything that has happened in my life that I had control over. I stopped taking all of the shame, guilt, and responsibility that belongs to others. I could not wash off the shame. I could not divorce shame. The only way I was able to stop the shameful behavior and get it out of my life was to confront it, find the root, and peel it away.

Learning something new or creating something is how I spend some of my days now. Spending time sorting out and organizing the last fifty-one years of mental sticky notes that are wedged in my brain is its own ongoing venture.

There are many gaps in my life that I can't account for—time that just seems to have evaporated. I can remember parts of my life as if they were yesterday, but there are entire years that I can't remember. The gaps may unfold in these pages, or they may never unfold; either way, I'm okay. It may seem like I'm jumping around, I'm not a writer and I write what comes up.

I may express feelings that might make some uncomfortable. If that happens to you, there is a reason. If it is more than just empathy, dig deeper.

I have two sons, Joshua and Daniel from my ex-husband Clinton Brown. They are the two greatest tributes to the best parts of me. I love who they are as people. My son Joshua has a master's degree in education and museum curation. He works in a museum. Joshua is also in the military. He is a medic and a national first responder. He is a born facilitator and educator. He is married to a beautiful, sweet woman, Eva. She is blond haired blue eyed and very beautiful. She has skin that is alabaster white. I love her big, beautiful smile. She will do anything for you because she has a beautiful heart.

My son Daniel is a talented art student in a private collage. He speaks Japanese. I am proud of both my boys. In spite of everything we've been through, we all move on with love and empathy. My boys and I are very close, even though we don't sit on the phone and chat for hours. We can count on each other no matter what.

My husband and best friend Don

My funny husband

Me in Grand Cayman learning new hard
lessons about charctorGP.

My oldest son and his wife on wedding day

My youngest son the Artist

My sons beautiful wife Eva I love so much

2
My Beautiful Scars

When I was two, I was badly burned. I had third-degree burns over 50 percent of my body. I spent fourteen days in a coma. I do not remember it happening, but this is what I'm told: There was a coffee pot on the kitchen table, the big kind with a spigot, because my mother drank coffee all day. I was playing under the kitchen table with my brother, and my mother pulled me out. I got caught on the cord, and the pot tipped over and I was burned. When they pulled my sleepers off, several layers of skin came off with it.

I do remember them cutting the skin off my ankle and elbow over and over. The doctors had to keep peeling back the skin because it healed over so quickly that it was still raw inside; they were afraid gangrene would set in. I had to wear all-white clothing so the dye would not cause infection.

I was tormented by kids at school because of my burns. The scars are ugly to most people, but not to me. The scars on the left arm neck and leg remind me that I am lucky to be alive. When I was younger, I would wear long-sleeved shirts all the time because I did not want to get teased.

We moved so frequently that it seemed as if I was always

making new friends wherever we would go. Everyone thought it was so easy for me to make friends, but really I just pushed the fear of rejection down. My feelings were something I shared with no one. I opened them up when I was alone so I could examine them. I spent a lot of my time in my head. I would analyze everything.

I would read the dictionary to help me sort things out. I would look up words like *hate*, *responsibility*, *integrity*, and *love*. Looking up all the things in my world helped me to understand and cope.

You would be surprised what happens when you read the definitions of everything you hear. This became a very useful tool for me as a child. My vocabulary was well above average. Between my dictionary and horribly abusive parents, I learned how to read people well and use powerful words to make my peers uncomfortable when they made fun of me because of my scars or tried to make me feel filthy because of my family.

Facing humiliation head-on gave me power, because it helped me to see that there is nothing anyone can do to me that I can't recover from. That is what courage means to me, and that is what I have tried to teach my sons.

3
It's Never Okay

My father was a pedophile. Yes, that's what it's called when you put your fingers in your daughter's vagina. It is never okay!

I don't know how old I was the first time I was abused. I know I was very young—no more than four. I just remember thinking, *Is this normal? Why is he doing this?* I was sitting on his lap. He took his finger, and through my underpants he put his finger in my rectum. I just kept thinking, *I don't like this, this hurts.*

At that time we lived in South San Francisco on Belmont Avenue. My father and I were sitting in a large, dark chair in the corner of the front room, away from the large picture window. I remember him whispering to me to go change my underpants.

When I was about six years old, my mother became pregnant with my sister. My mother would call her looney Lou, because her middle name is Louise. My mother hated my sister because she had had a difficult pregnancy. I knew there was something wrong with my mother, but no one would say what. It was like she sort of lost her cookies—as in crazy. The night she went into labor, my father took my mother to the hospital. My two older brothers and I were sent across the street to our neighbor Viola's house. I liked Viola.

It was very stormy that night. My father came home late and came across the street and got me but left my brothers. I wanted to stay with Viola and my brothers.

After we got home, my father penetrated me digitally. I was crying and combative, and he started yelling at me and then sent me to my room. I started heading to my room but then went into the kitchen and got a saucer and went to my parents' doorway and threw the saucer at my father. It shattered against the wall. The only other thing I remember from that evening was sitting at the big window in the front room watching the rain.

I shared a bedroom with my two older brothers. They had bunk beds on one side of the room, and I had a bed on the other side of the room under the window. There were trees by the window, and in stormy weather the branches would blow against the window and make scary noises.

I started getting out of bed in the middle of the night. I would hide in the closet and try to cover up under the junk and clothes. I could hear my own breathing. I'm sure it sounded louder to me than it actually was. I felt safe there.

After my sister was born, we moved. We moved a lot because my mother would end up hating everyone on the block. It would get so bad that adults were all fighting like school kids so we would move. I can't remember where, but I think it was to Hayward, California. My brothers, Peter and John, shared a room, and I shared my room with my sister. My mother had a dog, Domino. He was a German shepherd. She loved that dog more than she loved any of us, including her husband. Every dog she ever had became vicious. If anyone knocked on the door the dog would go crazy, barking and growling as if he was going to rip someone apart.

Everywhere we moved my mother would make friends

with all the teenage guys. She would bend over backward and do anything for them; it was weird. She was always involved in the lives of my brothers friends. There was a time in particular that bothered me because one of my brother John's friends Cory came to our house and asked my mother to hide a gun. I'm not sure what the gun was used for. I just remember it had something to do with stolen S&H Green Stamps and money from a gas station. My mother was always harboring someone or something from the police.

The next place we moved was to San Jose, to a house on Blossom Hill Boulevard. We had an above-ground pool in the backyard. I was in this pool the last time my father laid a hand on me. I was fooling around in the pool, pretending I was a diver in the ocean. My father got into the pool. He came over like he was going to pick me up and toss me in the air. I tried to get away but couldn't. He did not throw me in the air that time. He took his hand and pulled my swimsuit aside, and I felt his hand inside me.

I panicked. I wanted out of that pool. I broke away, hurried to the side, climbed the ladder, and fell from the top step backward onto the cement. I got up and ran into my room and slammed the door. My father was right behind me. He came into my room and asked if I was okay. I said, "Just get out."

That was the last time he touched me. I was about twelve I think. My room was my solace.

I was lying on my bed thinking about what had happened. I took a pocketknife and cut the word *NO* on my hip.

Every time I dug that knife into my skin, I would let out a silent scream inside. My mouth opened and nothing came out, but I heard it, and it felt good. I relate it to holding your breath until you can't hold it in any longer and you gasp to get all the air you can in to fill your lungs. Taking in the deep breath is such a relief. Welcome to cutting. I had no idea that's what it was called. It helped me get rid of some of the intense pain and anxiety. I found that i was not able to get rid of the anxiety any other way. For a while I relied on cutting as an outlet but soon realized it was too visible. I was suffering inside and I needed a way to get it to the outside before my insides consumed me.

One of the houses of hell where all of us
suffered in some form or another

4
I Wish You Were Never Born

As far back as I can remember my mother was a miserable woman. My brother Peter and I stuck together because my mother was overly attached to my brother John.

I never figured out why she favored him over Peter and me, but it was very obvious to the two of us and some of our relatives. She always tried to push him at everyone. My uncle (my mother's brother) James he would come over to visit frequently, and she would lock Peter and me in the garage for hours.

We would get so hungry that we would eat the Walter Kendall Fives dog food stored in the garage—a popular brand when we were kids. I can still taste the flavor of the green kibbles; trust me, they were definitely not the same as green M&M's! There were red ones, green ones, black ones, and brown ones. We ate jade plants and called them pickles. We would move all the old wooden backyard furniture together and pretend we were on a ship, sailing away. We spent many days thinking and planning our way out.

We were locked out for so long one time that I fell asleep on a rocking horse my grandfather had made. There was a nail sticking out of the neck of the horse, and it punctured my skin just above my belly button. I still have a scar from that nail on my stomach.

One morning my mother locked us out of the house when my uncle showed up to visit. Peter and I decided we were going to run away. We were maybe six and eight years old. I am amazed now to think about what we packed and where we went; we were well organized. We had everything that we needed.

Later that morning, we made our great escape. My brother Peter asked to come in to use the bathroom, and while he was in the house he got every penny from a small piggy bank. We packed up his pup tent, and I packed my doll and a doll bathtub so we could use it to wash our clothes. We were running away for good. We were not the kids that get one block down the street and an hour later are back home.

We pitched the pup tent behind the local grocery store. The market was across the street from the recreation park, where there were huge bathrooms and a sink. We used our change from the piggy bank to buy a loaf of bread and a pack of cheese. We had decided we would stay behind that store because there we would have access to food and water. We found a big box of unopened Tootsie Rolls behind the store receiving area. We had snacks, water, and a restroom. We were going to live forever behind that grocery store. I strolled through the store and ate some grapes and small pieces of candy.

I think one of the neighbors saw us and called our house, because that night my father came to get us. After we got home, no one bothered asking why we had run away; they just took our Tootsie Rolls and laughed at us. Part of our punishment was humiliation. I was so angry as I watched them eat our Tootsie Rolls and make fun of us. I thought, *Why did they even bother to come and get us? Really, they did not care but they did have to keep up appearances.* My father had everyone in stitches.

Throughout our childhood Peter and I were busy surviving and trying to escape a manic-depressive mother. My mother was a beater. She was never diagnosed, but I'm telling you she was manic-depressive (today it would be called bipolar). I think she was ashamed of whom she was and felt hopeless to do anything about it.

When I was seven, a relative gave me a pair of 14-karat gold post earrings shaped like turtles. I don't remember who gave them to me, but it was the only nice thing that was not taken away. I was so afraid that the backs would come off the post of one of the earrings and I would lose it that I kept pushing the backs tighter, until finally one lodged in my earlobe and stuck. When my mother found out, she beat me on the back of my head with my hairbrush. I hated those earrings after that. And I'm not that crazy about turtles.

My mother hated who she was so much that she punished everyone. It was easy for her to beat us because we were small and she could control us. My mother felt we took her life away. When she was in one of her many depressive times, she would make a tomato and mayonnaise sandwich, and if we watched her eat, she would start throwing shoes or anything she could get her hands on. She never wanted us to see her eat. My mother would chase one of us down, grab us by the hair, and shake the crap out of us.

She always claimed to have some kind of problem with her legs; I never knew what it was. I was told it was some kind of muscle disease but never knew for sure.

I am a survivor. By all rights I should not be here today. My mother suffered from mental illness, and my father was a pedophile. In all fairness, I did gain some positive attributes from living with my parents. I learned how to defend myself and how to achieve. Their sickness and shame influenced my life in many negative ways, and as a result my children's lives were influenced by my sickness and shame. But this is where it stops. We have a moral responsibility to ourselves and our families to break the chain. Moral responsibility is based on an accurate understanding of right and wrong, and an accurate understanding of right and wrong needs to come from knowledge.

I do not want another generation to carry on the shame and guilt. I'm telling my story of courage and triumph. We need to hear more such stories. Our world is filled with fear and anger. Sometimes life is unfair and seems hopeless. We do have the ability to choose to make change. We are stronger than we think we are. Strength gradually grows as we challenge ourselves by doing what scares us.

Some may find working with the computer daunting; for others it is finding your way, beginning in a new area. Do what scares you! You will see that vision or no vision, limb or no limbs, by sharing our stories of survival and courage openly we are able to move ahead and heal. Then we can help others find their courage. I got married way to young to a man I did not love. I had been treated so horribly growing up that I was willing to put many people in emotional danger and did not even know it. Clinton Brown, he was nice to me, he was weak and I married him.

My shame overcame my courage in the beginning. But when I looked at my kids, my heart ached, and I knew what I needed to do. I needed to push through my feelings of pain and face myself and my fears in a judgmental world. I had to stop feeling ashamed because my ex-husband molested kids. I was holding on to his shame. Once I could face myself I could face others.

My analogy: Overcoming shame is like a child learning to walk. Learn to stand holding onto something. Stand, get scared, let go, and fall. Then try it again, build confidence with encouragement from some source, then try again, and take a few steps. As we go through the process, we get stronger and more confident. Each time we try something, even if we fail, the attempt makes us stronger. We are more capable than we think we are. We are born without shame, innocent. As innocent children, we receive our parents' unresolved shame.

The family is the child's only contact until he or she starts interacting with daycare, school, other families, and friends. Even an infant can pick up on signals of shame, and that shame grows and spreads. My parents acted shamefully, and I felt ashamed. My parents were very dishonest, and I felt like a liar. My parents stole things, and I felt like a thief. Those seeds were planted and grew into horrible decisions based on shame, guilt, and lies. I deserve to feel at peace, and so does every person seeking it. I want to help others find their strength and courage through situations that seem hopeless.

I did not have anyone to teach me courage. I had to put my ego aside. I had to feel how I felt. I know that sounds weird, but I had to stop and walk myself through the process of each emotion, taking each painful link off my chain because it did not belong to me. My children deserve to have peace and privacy in their lives. I have a gift—courage and compassion— and I want to help anyone who truly needs help.

5
Growing Pains

When I was in high school, my brother Peter moved out, and I would sneak out to go see him. One day when I got home from visiting him, my mother was sitting as usual at the table with a cup of coffee in her hand—no matter what hour of the day, it was a cup of coffee and a cigarette. The first words out of her mouth were, "Did you see that son of a bitch?"

She started yelling, and I just walked away; I did not care anymore. She grabbed me by the back of the hair and slapped me in the face. I held my tears back. I just stared at her, not giving her any satisfaction. For God's sake, I was just a kid. Trying to make a crazy person see logic was a worthless effort. I could not wait to grow up and get away. Negativity filled my brain, and I brought that everywhere I went. It is sad that someone else's compulsions and weaknesses can destroy the innocence of three generations.

My parents lost their house on Grey Ghost Drive in San Jose, California. They have lost every house they've ever had. When my father moved us north to Weimar Ca, I was devastated. From San Jose to some podunk town! That is what

I thought of all the trees and roads with no sidewalks. It was a bit of a shock.

I was used to having to make new friends because we moved so much. I think I went to four or five different elementary schools. When the school would start asking questions, my mother would start badgering my father to move. I just did not want to move so far away. It was a blow. Yet I made friends quickly and tried to make the best of it.

I made some friends at Holly Acres Detention Center in Applegate, California. Ray and Laura were a couple I met there. Another friend I made there was Lee—I don't remember his last name. I had a crush on him, but I never told anyone.

Holly Acres was a detention home for kids from all over California. It had a dormitory-style setup. Sometimes I would get off the bus to go home with my friends. I think the detention counselors knew something was not right, because they let me go on trips with them, and I would go there on the weekends whenever I could get away from my mother. They would have a barbecue and play softball in the field nearby.

I wished I could live there. I asked the counselors how I could get permission to move there. They said, "You don't want to be here. It is one thing to visit, but you don't belong here."

At the time I took it as a rejection. I was hurt because I felt I would have thrived in that environment.

Looking back on it today, I think the counselors were right—I did not belong there. I was not a trouble maker or a runaway. I was just the opposite. I never wanted to get in trouble.

My best friend Beth lived next door. We went to Colfax High School together. We did not hang out a lot at school; she hung with kids a couple years ahead. I had a crush on her handsome brother Kevin. We would flirt back and forth a little. In the summer we would all go out in the dark and hang out trying to scare each other because there were no streetlights.

One evening Kevin and I went down to Harry's Bar. Harry's Bar served food, so minors were allowed to go in. There was an old bus bench next to the bar, and we sat down to talk. I was excited to see him. He said I was so sweet. He kissed me, I felt special for about a millisecond.

Then the tape of crap started playing in my head. I felt horribly uncomfortable. He put his hands up the back of my shirt, trying to undo my bra. I pulled away quickly, and he tried to hang onto me but I pushed him away. I jumped up and said I had to go. I ran up the hill to my house.

What Kevin did not know was that my bra straps were sewn together because I only had one bra and it was so tight I had to sew the back closed. I was ashamed.

Even though Beth and Kevin came from a messed-up, alcoholic family, they still had what I considered luxuries and a lavish lifestyle. I often thought about what it would be like to have things that you needed—stupid things like underwear, bras, towels, and toothpaste.

I hated PE in school, not because it was exercise but because I did not wear underwear. I only had one pair, which I tried to save for that time of the month. I would steal paper towels from the bathroom at school and roll them up because I did not have any sanitary products. At other times I used cut-up T-shirts. I learned to smile through everything; I hid all my pain inside.

I have always tried to find reason in everything that happens. *What was the motivation that led to this or that?* When I analyze everything, it occupies my mind, and I don't feel so empty. I'm busy in my head sorting. I need to understand why people do what they do. This was always my way of coping with my anxiety. When it became harder to focus my thoughts, I would become depressed and, at times, suicidal. To me, life seemed to be something to endure.

I was about thirteen years old when my father quit his job to become his own boss. He bought a beater Ford truck spotted with primer and big ugly wooden sides that were half broken. He was now in the scrap metal business.

Early one summer morning my father opened my bedroom door and said, "Get dressed. You're going to help me today."

I was not sure what that meant. I got up and got dressed in a pair of blue jean overalls my friend Rene had given me; they were cool at the time. The shirt I was wearing was white T-shirt material with small pink roses on it that I had found in the physical education lost-and-found. I did not have PE clothes, and my teacher said to get something from the box so I could go to my next class and not be all sweaty. I did not return the shirt; I really liked it. I had long hair, almost waist length. I'm not being conceited here, but I was very pretty.

I headed out the front door and there it was: the scrap metal hauling truck, dented from pillar to post. I climbed up into the smelly cab praying to be invisible. Our first stop was a muffler shop. My father told me to go around the back of the building and start loading the old mufflers. I was frantically thinking, *What? Do what?* I had no idea this was what we were going to do. I felt like such a gross, disgusting pig. At fourteen years old, coming from this screwed-up family, my self-perception was shameful in every way.

Primarily men worked at the stops we went to. My father created regular stops to pick up their scrap metals. When I would get out of the truck, some of the employees of the auto body shops would make very inappropriate comments. How often do you see a girl picking up scrap metal? I've never seen another one.

My father would say, "Start loading the scrap metal—I'll be right back." There was always someone he had to go see, or he had to go to the bathroom. I would get stuck loading the truck.

I busted my butt that first day, and that was one of many to come. It was a hot summer day, and I had to help my father go junking. By the time we got home that evening, I was tired, and I'd had enough. When I went into the bathroom to shower, I took a pair of scissors, put my hand on the bathroom counter, and stabbed the scissors into my hand in the meaty part between the thumb and index finger of my right hand. I did not let out a peep. It hurt so badly, but now my father would have to do his own work. Today, I feel sad for that sad young girl I was.

I regularly played pool for money at Harry's Bar, hoping to make enough to buy food at school the next day. I was at Harry's one evening and saw a guy enter the bar. I found out his name was Derrick. He and I played pool, and I beat him. I thought he was cool. He was twenty-three; I was almost sixteen.

We started seeing each other. He was the bad-boy type, sometimes, but I was attracted to him. When he was nice, he was fun to hang out with. I was still a virgin, but Derrick did not believe me. I think he made it a quest to conquer me when I look back on it. Derrick would say he would call me, and he would not call.

He started seeing a friend of mine. I was hurt. Derrick said he was seeing Reta just as a friend. He came by my house to invite me to a Thanksgiving party at the house he shared with his brother David. He told me that he wanted me to go, but he was not going to bring me home. I said I was not worried. I had no clue what I was doing.

It was 1975; I was fifteen years old at a party at a house filled with people who were all in their mid to late twenties. I had no business being there. They were drinking and smoking pot. I only smoked cigarettes. I never wanted to be out of control—being impaired in my house was not safe. Derrick told me to have some eggnog; there was just a touch of whiskey in it. I took a big sip, and it tasted terrible. Derrick told me I was beautiful, and I just sat there. I thought, *I'm just going to give in and see where this goes.*

Well, we ended up having sex. It hurt, and I bled all over the place. I was so ashamed. His hands were full of blood, and he passed out. I could hear people in the garage playing pool and partying. I tried to wake Derrick up, but he would not wake up. I got up and turned on the light. I was terrified. It looked like someone had been shot—blood was everywhere.

I grabbed my clothes and went into the bathroom. Every time I stood up, I would bleed heavily. I was scared because I had no idea I was going to bleed like that. I thought I was bleeding to death.

I went into the kitchen and got a jar from the cupboard and filled it with water. I went back into the bedroom and tried to clean Derrick's hands off. His brother came and woke him up and asked what had happened. Derrick said, "I popped her cherry."

Derrick went out to the garage and started bragging about it. I wanted to die, I was so humiliated. I did not know one of the guys at the party named Clint, but he came up to me and asked if he could give me a ride home. I said yes, please.

I had my sweater tied around my waist because my pants were covered in blood. When Clint dropped me off, I walked through the front door to the house. My parents were up; it was four in the morning. They asked where I had been, but I just didn't bother to answer. I figured if they wanted to beat me or ground me, I did not care. I just walked straight to my room. I stayed in my room for two days.

I was waiting for them to start yelling and screaming, and I was going to just leave if they started anything, but they didn't. I was at my lowest point when Clint came by the weekend after Thanksgiving. He would call every few days to see how I was.

One day, he asked me if I wanted to get something to eat. I said sure, and we went out. We soon became very close. I trusted him because he was nice to me, but in actual fact what he was doing was grooming me. He was a sick man. He was twenty-five, nine years my senior. I was sixteen—way too young to be with this person. But I did not know any better.

6
The In-Betweens

I stood at the door of the Nazarene Church in Auburn, California. The sun was bright and warm on my face. I was about to walk through the doors into a hell I had never envisioned.

I married Clinton Eugene Brown on April 29, 1978. I did not love him—I did not know what love was. My mistake was thinking that if someone was nice to me that I owed him. I did feel as if I owed him something, because he had been kind to me and he had given me food and shelter and freedom. He was oddly familiar. He made me feel as if I could control my own life. I was very wrong.

Now that I'm grown, I have had time to reflect a bit. Wow! I can't believe how naive I was in the ways of the world.

Clint and I dated for a few months before he asked me to marry him. I ignored my intuition—I did not follow my instincts. He told me that he had been married before and that his wife had died. I felt horrible because I really did not want to marry him, but I did. Then after we were married he told me he had lied: he had never been married. When he told me that, I felt as if I had been hit in the face with a frying pan.

A few months later I found out I was pregnant. When the doctor told me I was pregnant, I could not think. It was like the experience was not real. As I progressed in my pregnancy, Clint would go out drinking and spend all of our money. It was not a good situation. We got into a pattern: he would not come home from work but would go out with his friends and drink. I would just worry and look for him.

My pregnancy was pretty easy. No morning sickness, no problems physically. I was just trying to cope with all the lies. I went into labor at 7:30 in the morning on January 11, 1979. Joshua was born January 12 at 9:22 a.m. I thought—or rather, hoped—that Clint would step up. I was wrong.

During the next three years of our marriage I spent much of my time trying to manage Clint instead of being a mom. Finally, I left Clint and moved up to Washington to get away from him. I was just so sick of the crap. I wanted out. I kept asking myself, *Why is my life like this?* I just wanted to disappear—not true, I wanted *him* to disappear.

I had been in Washington for about a week, and Clint was calling and promising me he would change. I was under a lot of pressure. My Joshua was a handful at three years old, and I thought I should try to work things out for his sake—at least try.

I came back to California, to our two-story house in Rocklin. About six weeks after I returned home, I got sick, and I kept getting sick. It turned out that I was eight to ten weeks pregnant. I made them do the test multiple times because I had been on the pill. But sometimes the pill does not work. I have a son to prove it.

This pregnancy was stressful. I was stuck with no car and a three-year-old. I sold things to get money for diapers and food. I remember one night in particular when I was eight and a half months pregnant. I was calling all over trying to track Clint down, and he was nowhere to be found.

He finally came home about 2:30 a.m., very drunk. He

started up the staircase, falling all over the place—he couldn't walk. I picked him up and carried him up the stairs because I did not want Joshua to see his father like that.

When we got to the top of the stairs, Clint opened the closet door, lifted the lid on the hamper, and started peeing in it. I was so mad.

I got him out of the closet and tried to get him to the toilet, but he was so out of it, he just kept going to the staircase. While I was trying to empty the hamper, he went to the top stair and started peeing on the stairs. I was pissed. I got him into the bathroom, where he passed out.

I was so angry that I picked up my stiff-bristle brush and hit him so hard in the back that the bristles stuck in his back. In the morning Clint told me that he had little holes in his back. He did not remember anything—nothing.

Daniel was born on March 20, 1983. It had been a very difficult pregnancy. I was sick a lot, and I was overdue by forty-three days. Daniel was a very big baby, over ten pounds. They induced my labor, and I was in labor for about fourteen hours. The placenta pulled away from the uterus, and I started hemorrhaging, so I was given an emergency C-section.

When I woke up, groggy and out of it, I was told I had a beautiful, big baby boy. When I finally got to see Daniel, he had an IV in his foot, and they had shaved the sides of his head because he needed to have IVs in his scalp as well. He had a ton of hair, and the shaving gave him a baby Mohawk. I loved it.

His heart had stopped during the C-section. He still has a murmur. I was in the hospital for almost a month. Clint came to see me at the hospital, and he had been drinking. I became quite depressed. I had a new baby, a four-year-old, and an alcoholic husband. I was at my lowest—or so I thought.

By the time I got back on my feet, I had decided to leave Clint. I took my sons and went back to Washington. Clint followed me; he wanted to try to start over in a new place. I got a job right away working in collections for Thousand Trails

Campgrounds. Clint was unemployed—he never really tried to get work.

One day about six months later, my boss came over to my desk and said he wanted to talk to me. I couldn't figure out what was wrong. My boss walked me down the long hallway to the smoking lounge. I was a smoker then. My boss lit a cigarette for me. He said the sitter had called and wanted him to tell me that my husband had picked up my oldest son. She did not know where he was going.

Where was he going? All I could do was think of all the things that could happen. I hurried home and booked a flight for Sacramento. I went to his mother's house in Auburn, northeast of Sacramento, and he was there. He said he would not give my son to me unless I stayed and tried to work on things. I had to move in with him and his mother something I did not want to do but I had my son back. He held me hostage with my kids.

Over time this sort of thing started to wear on me. Going back and forth—it was awful.

I felt like I was a horrible mother. I wanted more for my boys. There were many times when I was overwhelmed and felt as if I was drowning in responsibility. I was stuck at home, well aware of a pattern of leave, go get drunk, come back home.

One of the many times Clint went out drinking and did not come home, I got a call around five in the morning from the police department. Clint had been in an accident. He had driven our car off a freeway overpass. He ran from the car with only one shoe on, knowing that if the police could not find him then they could not do a blood alcohol test. He did not want a DUI on his record.

Clint had called some friends to come and get him, and the friends also called me. The police traced the car registration and came to the house looking for Clint because they found beer in the car. I told them where he was, but they could not charge him with DUI because a blood alcohol test had not been administered.

I had been feeling ill—not quite right. I could not put my finger on it. I was very tired, irritable, and weak. Just not right. I made an appointment with my doctor.

They took some blood tests. They also did a Pap test and a mammogram. I had forgotten my insurance card and promised to run it by, but I never did.

The doctor's office called my emergency contact at work and left a message for me to come in ASAP. I arrived ready to bitch at them for harassing me for my card. The receptionist told me that they had called because some of my results had come back abnormal. I asked what "abnormal" meant, but the receptionist just said they wouldn't know anything until they got my full results back.

I had an appointment the next day. They took some biopsies and said they would let me know. I was very nervous because no one in the doctor's office would say what they thought it might be. I got the results about a week later. I had micro-invasive carcinoma of the uterus and cervix.

My doctor said I needed to think about what I wanted to do. If I had a hysterectomy as recommended, I would not be able to have any more children. I decided to go ahead with the surgery. Within four weeks I was healed enough from the biopsies that they could go forward with surgery. I had the hysterectomy, and they were able to get all the cancer. But it started me thinking about how short life could be. I was not happy; I could not stay with Clint.

Once I recovered from the surgery, I started to reevaluate my priories. My kids were the most important.

I started carefully planning to leave Clint. He suspected something, I think, because I was not fighting back when he tried to engage me. He quietly took both the boys and put them in my old Bronco and took off. I did not see which direction he went. For a while I just sat in my living room waiting and worrying, sick to my stomach. I had no idea if he was going to hurt them or leave them somewhere. I feared he would get drunk and have an accident.

Clint brought the boys back home around midnight. He carried them in and put them in bed. I went to bed, waiting for him to pass out. He tried to force me to have sex, but I started punching him and pushed him off with my legs. He finally passed out. I went into the kitchen and got out a few grocery bags and put some clothes in them for the boys. I carried Joshua out to the truck and locked the door.

I went back in to get Daniel. I scooped him up, and out the door I went with him. On my way back in to get the clothing, my mother-in-law tried to stop me. She grabbed my arm, and I pulled away. She yelled, "I'm going to go and wake Clint, and we will see who gets those kids." She was inches from my face.

I screamed back, "Go ahead, wake him up—that's a joke. Your son, you must be so proud."

She slapped me in the face twice. I wanted to beat her freaking head in, but I knew what she was doing. I trusted my intuition enough to walk away. *Don't say a word just walk away,* I told myself. She would have called the police and claimed that I hit her. I had to concentrate on getting out.

I left the house and went to a hotel. I put the kids in bed and sat and made a plan. I needed to get away from California, away from my mother-in-law, away from Clint, and away from all that crap.

I decided I would go to the police and tell them what had happened. So early the next morning I drove with the kids to the police station and asked them to help me get my kids' clothes and a few things from my home. I made them aware of the situation. I was afraid to go back to the house alone because I thought I may get pushed into doing something I would regret and loose my kids. The police thought it would be a good idea to escort me. I told the police, "I just want to get my kids out of this. They should not have to go through this."

The police followed me—the kids riding with them—to the house. They pulled up a few houses away from mine. I parked in front of my house. I went up the walkway to the front door with one of the officers while the boys waited in the police car. He stepped to the side, and I tried to open the door. My mother-in-law had put the chain lock on and looked through the top part of the door. She saw me and shook her head from side to side. She said, "No, you're not getting in."

But when the officer tapped on the glass with his club, she was apologizing all over the place. She tried the "I'm old and frail, and she scares me" routine.

The cop said, "I think I have a pretty good idea of what is going on here." He told me to take my time, that there was no rush, but I just wanted to get out of there. I loaded clothes for us and some of their toys and their bikes. The police wished me good luck, and the boys and I got into the car and headed north. I had a long time to think on that drive to Washington.

My brother had bought an old farm-style house in Washington—by house I mean shiplap walls and no plumbing. It was a house but not inhabitable. Peter and I started working on it—sewer, power, sheet rock, tape, and texture. We put a roof on. We worked every spare minute to fix it up so the boys and I could live there.

It was kind of a scary house. It was filled with what had to be fifty years of hoarded magazines and trash. The outside of the house was cedar shingles that were weather-beaten to a weathered white that had turned black in spots. The house was not level. We rented house jacks, crawled under the house, jacked it up on one end, and pounded the shims in to level it. We got most of the house sheet rocked and the bathroom installed. We had a wood-burning stove.

As I lay in my bed, I could hear a ruffling sound in the

walls. I was not sure what it was, so I just closed my eyes and tried to focus on something else. I slept in the living room, and one bedroom was finished for the boys. The other bedroom was filled with tools, wood, sheet rock, and paint. The upstairs was closed off because it was still a mess.

Since we lived in a rural area, I thought the sounds might have been raccoons. I thought wrong, it was not raccoons. It was mice. I know this because I got up and went into the kitchen, and there they were scurrying over my counter and stove. I was too tired to be scared. To deal with it, I set traps, but that kind of sucked because the traps needed to be cleaned. It was disgusting, but I got over it.

I had become very thin. In fact, I hit my lowest weight yet at eighty-five pounds. I would eat a bran muffin in the morning and yogurt for dinner and either go to the gym or work on my house. Daniel was now five and Joshua nine. I had never filed for divorce, so legally Clint and I were still married. My sons were sad that they did not have a "regular family."

One morning after Daniel had gotten ready for school, I found him sitting out on the porch crying. He said, "Mom, I don't want to divorce Dad. Maybe we could get him help." That broke my heart.

When the boys' father was in their lives, they were always on edge, waiting for the wheels to come off his cart. He was now living with a woman from his work. That spring my sons wanted to spend the summer with their dad. He promised me he would let me come and get them if I wanted to. He said he would enjoy the chance to try to make it up to our boys. I did not trust this, but I took the boys to visit him.

The woman Clint was living with had one child, a daughter. That's all I knew about her. So I stayed close for a few days to make sure I could trust them to care for my kids, and then I went back up to Washington.

My kids were with their dad for a week, and then they wanted to come back home. The following week I drove down to Auburn to pick them up. Clint wanted to talk to me about moving closer to the boys. He wanted to move up to Washington.

He said, "I'm sorry, I know I've said that before, but I mean it this time. I miss you, I miss the boys. I want to try to make things right."

I felt so horrible about everything that I stayed for eight days to try to sort things out. I asked Clint about the woman he was living with. He said she was just sharing the rent. I knew it was bullshit, but my youngest would cry and ask me not to be a divorced family because all his friends' families were, and they were always sad. I said okay. Clint said he wanted my oldest son to stay, and I could take Daniel back to Washington with me.

My kids wanted this last chance to try to have a relationship with their dad. How could I look those boys in the eye and say no? I left Clint to move to Washington, and I tried to make it work. In my heart I felt something tugging at me. Something was not right, but I brushed it off as awkward distance, so much time apart. I tried so hard to make it work. When something is not right and your intuition talks to you, please, please—listen to it.

7
The Ground Starts to Shake

I purchased the farmhouse from my brother Peter at Christmas 1991. I worked third shift at Boeing, and Clint got a job with the Auburn School District in Washington as a custodian. He worked morning to afternoon, and he would be home at night. So I would sleep when I got home in the morning because I had to be at work for the night shift at 10:30 p.m.

One weekend my seven year old niece Melissa came over for tje weekend. At the end of the weekend, when Clint took her home, he wasn't even back yet from dropping her off before my brother called me. He said Melissa had told him that Clint touched her private parts when she was sitting on his lap at the computer. He asked us to come over and talk about it.

Clint denied it. He said, "She was on my lap, and she was squirming around, and she pinched my leg, and I was just trying to adjust positions."

I knew he was lying, and when we got home, I told him so, "If this ever, *ever* happens again, I will do everything I can to make sure you go to jail. I swear it."

About a month or so passed, and my niece Ramona came to visit for the weekend. Before I left for work Sunday night, I put her in my bed. Clint was going to move her to the couch when he was ready for bed.

The next afternoon, I awoke to the phone ringing. It was my brother. He told me that Clint had molested my other niece who is six, Ramona, and she had told the school administrators, who called the police. He was arrested and held while the police investigated the claims.

The police came to the house and took statements from every family member. They started digging through his past and had more questions. They gave him a polygraph test, but it was inconclusive. After three days they let him out of jail on his own recognizance because he was being cooperative. I was inconsolable, in shock. *No, don't let him out!*

The school district put him on a paid leave of absence, so, of course, he got to stay home and drink.

At one point I handed Clint my .357 Magnum and a bottle of Vicodin. I said, "Just kill yourself. Do us all a favor, just kill yourself." I told him not to shame his kids—just do it. He was a coward. He said he would do it but chickened out.

It was like being hit in the head with a hammer. All I could do was just sit and stare at the paneling in my bedroom. I was beating myself up over what Clint did. I kept asking myself, *Why didn't I see this? How could I not know?* I just wanted him gone.

I begged him, "Please leave, leave this state, and leave us alone."

He kept saying, "I'm afraid."

I wanted to kill him—I truly did because I was so distraught. I had no words. He said he would leave town. I told him to go back to California.

After about a week, he did go back to the woman he had been living with in California. But he had abused her daughter too. So she told him to go back to Washington, or she would call the police. The Seattle police had already contacted his old employer in California. He was being investigated. After about five weeks he returned to Washington.

During all this, Clint had given me fifty dollars here and there, but he was falling apart. Finally, about three months after his arrest, I went to a lawyer and filed for divorce. In the divorce papers I put down that we shared no children together. I didn't ask for anything from him.

My ex-mother-in-law passed away and was cremated before Clint was convicted of child molestation. He did not want his mothers ashes that I had paid $700 for. I ended up having to pay the rest of her medical bills and her nursing home bills because Clint and I were still legally married.

Clint's mother had lung cancer, and during her treatment he had authorized expenditures like $600 for cabulance trips to take to her cancer treatments. I had to pay off all of those bills along with Clint's credit card bills and a loan for $22,000. I did not want to pay, but the judge said that although Clint owed those bills, I was the one with the house. The creditors would put a lien on my house, and I could lose it. So I took on his debt.

Our divorce was finalized ninety days after I filed, and I was glad. I took out a loan and paid all of the those bills.

During the sentencing and divorce, I took some time off work. It took me about two weeks to get myself together so I could go back to work. I can honestly say that something in me broke. I felt it. I can't explain it, but I felt something break inside. I think I was teetering on the edge of a nervous breakdown. I just kept telling myself things would be okay. All I needed to do was get back on schedule. Get back on task. I can do this. Don't look at the pile, just look at the shovel.

My first night back to work I took my lead into an office and told him everything that had happened. I told him I wanted him to keep it confidential. He said, "I'm sorry for your family." I was so ashamed to even say the words.

My lead told me to take all the time I needed, but I said, "I'm ready to come back. I need my routine back."

When I came in the next night, my boss was there, and he said he wanted to talk to me. I asked him what about. He said that people were talking about me and what had happened. He had told them to stop talking about me.

I was horrified and humiliated, and I wanted to die—I really did. I had to walk into a staff meeting and face all three shifts of my fellow coworkers who knew what had happened. I think my sister-in-law (who also worked for Boeing) decided to blab about what had happened.

I held my head high and poured myself into my work. I went from being distraught for two weeks to kicking ass at work. It did get easier. Shock and pain were moving to anger now. I was determined to confront the gossipers and judgers by confronting it head on, but that took its toll on me, and the anger turned inward. I developed a serious eating disorder. This made me feel strong when I felt weak. It became my way of redirecting my anxiety and punishing myself at the same time. I became a size 0.

My eating disorder had become my perfect punishment, because everyone just reaffirmed my behavior by saying reinforcing things: "You look fantastic." "Man, you lost a lot of weight." "Wow, you look like a different person." This helped me take some of the shame away, because I got a lot of positive feedback. This made being pathetic feel less pathetic.

I tried a support group for people with eating disorders, which was actually a food addiction group. The local hospital held the meetings twice a week. I arrived a bit late to the first meeting, so everyone turned to look at me as I opened the door. As I sat in a chair and listened, I realized this was not the right place for me. I was a waif, and everyone there was very large. The look I was getting was, *Why are you here?* I thought to myself, *There is no place I belong, no place I fit in.*

I had to overcome the anorexic lifestyle. My hair was

falling out, and I often felt light-headed and dizzy. People were beginning to comment now on my weight loss in a negative way: "You're too thin." "Are you eating?" "What have you eaten today?" I was so sick of hearing it. I knew I had to change something, because I physically couldn't carry on.

I found bulimia as a solution quite by accident. I had gotten the flu and as I was throwing up my yogurt and bran muffin, I thought, *This is it, this is perfect, because people will see me eating and stop nagging my ass. They will stop telling me I look too thin.*

And people learned to leave me alone. That whole thing was all about having some sort of personal power over something, because everything was so messed up. When I found out one of my coworkers had been gossiping about me, I just walked right up to her in front of everyone and said, "You have been talking about me and my family. Why don't you focus a little of your extra energy at the gym, because you are a fat pig. Mind your own life."

She weighed about two hundred and fifty pounds, and that was a mean thing to say, but I was hurt and angry. I did not find anything about it pleasurable. If someone told me he or she had a family crisis, I would do everything I could to help that person and his or her family. Unfortunately, not everyone thinks that way.

My brother was opening an antique store in a small town in Washington. I would go to work at the Boeing third shift, leaving for work as usual around 10:30 p.m. I would get home in time the next morning to get my kids' breakfast and leave for the antique store. I would open the store at 9:00 a.m., and my brother would take over between 4:00 and 4:30 p.m.

I would get back home, cook, and go over the day with the kids and help them with homework—that kind of thing. I would sleep for a few hours in the chair in my living room. Then I would get up and do it all again.

I followed this routine for quite a while—it helped me

make ends meet. I had a yard sale to get rid of stuff I did not need. I also would work two weekends a month, and the Boeing overtime helped me a lot. I had been trying to go to school and get my AA degree, but I'd had to withdraw every time the shit hit the fan with Clint.

There was a woman at another building at Boeing whose daughter knew my kids, and she was a gossiper. I told her, "If I hear gossip, and this hurts me or my kids, you will see a side of me that you will not like. And if you are taking this as a threat, you should, because it is. Mind your business." Taking control of the gossip was a high priority for me.

One afternoon my brother came into the antique store early and said I could go and get some sleep. I was exhausted. I went home and got into bed, and I was all warm and snugly. I guess I had been asleep for a few hours, when all of a sudden I opened my eyes, and Clint was standing in the middle of my living room. He was out on bail and had broken in. I told him to get out or I would call the police.

Clint said that he had no place to go. I screamed, "I don't care, you have no place here. You are so messed up! Leave! Get out!"

He got in his car and sat in my driveway for about twenty minutes. Then he peeled out of my driveway, throwing gravel everywhere.

His court date finally came, he was given a twelve-month jail sentence minus time served, mandatory counseling, and probation for five years. He was to have no contact with minors, not even his own children.

Soon after he went to jail, he began writing letters to me. I did not respond to any of them. Then the letters to my sons started arriving every few days. I had to intercept the mail because he was not supposed to have contact. The letters to my sons started out with how much he missed them. He said he was sorry that we were all sick liars.

The letters gradually became more angry and quite

threatening. Clint wrote that there was a conspiracy against him, that the police had framed him, and that the judge was out to get him. He was losing control.

Letters started arriving written in childlike handwriting, messy, with very large characters. Clint believed I was in on the conspiracy against him. That was really freaky. I saved all of the letters. The last letter I received stated that all the people who framed him would be identified when he got out. These were children he was writing to. Did he honestly believe I would let my children read the letters? What a moron.

I took a position at a Boeing plant closer to my home, so that was a plus. There, I became friendly with Don, a coworker I had known for several years. He was cool, and I enjoyed his company. He was my only friend in that cesspool of gossip and backstabbing we called work. Don and I were becoming close, but I did not want my work involved with my private life.

Finally, I agreed to go on a date with Don. We were inseparable from that first date. I was so excited—I had never been in love before. I felt loved by him. One evening I went over to his apartment, and I had my computer bag with me. I said, "I have something I want to talk to you about, Don. In this bag are letters from my ex-husband."

I took the letters from the bag and set them on the couch. I said, "You can end our relationship now if this is too hard for you. I understand completely—honestly, I do, so if you do, I would not blame you. I have a bit more drama than most."

Don looked at the letters and said, "I'm here with you."

My insides were all knotted up. Don had said that I was worth it. I felt as if Snoopy was dancing in my head. *I'm worth it.*

Oh yes, the letters. I took all those letters, and I went to the prosecutor's office. The prosecutor and I discussed the problem, and then I brought out the bag of letters. I told her that I was fearful because the letters were getting threatening, and he was sending them to my kids. The prosecutor said that even though he was in counseling, part of his sentence was to have no contact with minors. The prosecutor could see that the addresses on the labels were addressed to my sons, and she read every letter. She said that Clint fit the profile of a sociopath.

Clint had a progress report court date coming up. When the court date arrived, the court officers walked Clint into the courtroom. I was sitting in the courtroom with Don. My brother and his wife were also there. Clint saw me and said, "Hey, Beck," and then he called out to my brother by his nickname. He actually thought we were there to get him out.

The judge asked Clint if he had attended the counseling. His reply was yes. The judge asked if he had been following the rules about contact with minors, and again he said yes. The judge said, "Well, I have a whole bag of letters here that are addressed to children."

The judge read some of the contents of the letters. The judge told Clint that he was not going to confirm the twelve-month sentence, but was imposing the maximum time allowed. He gave him eight years with no time off for good behavior.

I felt as if I had done the right thing. I felt horrible when I told my boys about bringing the letters to the police, but I thought they needed to know.

I moved on. I spent years in therapy. I just needed somebody to listen, and I needed to talk about some of the traumas I'd encountered and how they affected my life.

8
My Private Shame

As I lay down in bed there are many times that I really did not want to wake up. There were many times I felt utterly alone.

When my ex-husband was charged with two counts of felony child molestation, I was in shock. I would get such bad headaches that my doctor gave me a prescription for Fioricet with codeine (a strong pain reliever for migraine). I could fill it every thirty days for one year at a time. One night, there were nineteen capsules left in the bottle, and I took them all. I just wanted to go to sleep. All the pain this situation was causing everyone was more than I could bear. It was so painful.

After a while, I was completely unaware of whether it was day or night. I just remember seeing my two boys sitting on my bed. I think that image of them is what brought me back. I poured myself into my work. T

I did get remarried, his name is Don. I love him with my whole self. When Don comes up and asks for a hug and kiss, I sink into his chest, and I feel comfort and safety. I have never felt that before; it makes my hard edges much softer. That soft feeling is like floating on a cloud of warm steam inside my body. I love the way Don smells and how he laughs at my sick sense of humor. I love his heart's energy. We give to each other, and we deserve each other.

He can be a bit misunderstood. What may seem like frankness to him, sometimes can be misinterpreted and seem like arrogance, which is not the case. He is a kind and loving man. Don gave me love, he gave me room, he understands me, and he lets me be me. We were married on November 14, 1997.

I am legally blind. I am often asked what that means. Well, it means I am blind in one eye and can't see out of the other.

Normally I would find the cliché annoying, but it's true. I am blind in my left eye, with light perception only. I have lost over half of the vision in my right eye. The condition that caused damage to and atrophy of my optic nerves is called pseudotumor cerebri. My body produces too much spinal fluid, resulting in increased pressure in the skull, with resulting compression headaches. The brain presses against the skull and crushes the optic nerves.

I have had very bad migraines since I was eight years old. Recently, I found out from my doctor that the headaches were probably not migraines, but were most likely compression headaches. I had surgery on my right eye in August 2009, undergoing a procedure called optic nerve sheath fenestration.

In this surgery, slits were cut in the sheath of the optic nerve so the excess spinal fluid could drain into my body. I take medication three times a day to remove the fluid. This disease can also be treated by putting shunts at the base of the brain to drain off the fluid.

I was losing vision so rapidly that my doctor said we needed to do the operative procedure right away. The morning of the surgery I was nervous, thinking *What if something goes wrong?* Then I will have no vision at all.

My doctor told me not to worry; he'd done the procedure

many times. It was nice of him to attempt to reassure me, but it did not help my anxiety. I was lying in a bed waiting to be wheeled into the operating room, and one of the surgical nurses came in and put a blanket on me that inflated with warm air all around my body. It was very comforting. A few moments later the sedation medication they put in my IV starting working. I remember trying to stay awake as long as I could—just in case things did not go as expected.

Thankfully, everything went well. I have not lost any more of my vision since the surgery, but I do have good days and bad days.

I have a guide dog named Dot. She is a beautiful Golden / Lab cross. I also have two miniature Pomeranians, Foxy and Fratello. I call Dot my Department of Transportation. I love to stroke her soft, freshly groomed hair: it smells like baby powder. Dot works when my anti-anxiety medication doesn't. I'm joking, but not only is she a great guide dog, she is my very best friend. She knows all my quirks, and I know hers. We mutually respect them.

Dot came from Guide Dogs for the Blind in San Rafael, California. She is an incredible gift. I am so lucky to have her. I have also acquired some new family members along with Dot. Dot's puppy raisers live close by, so she can see them often. They took care of her from the time she was eight weeks old and taught her basic obedience and manners. They socialized her with many other animals until she was old enough to begin guide dog training.

I am often asked the question, "How long have you been training your dog?"

I respond, "I'm not training the dog."

People just don't know what to say. I had one gentleman—I'm using the term loosely—ask me about training. When I gave my standard answer, he asked rudely, "Then what is the dog for?"

Now I must say that most of the time I am quite polite and

take incidents like this as an opportunity to educate. However, at times I may be having a bad day, and I'm not so nice; this was one of those days. My reply was, "My dog is for sniffing out assholes, and she just found another one. Good girl." Then we swiftly passed by. People can't fathom that not all blind people look like Stevie Wonder.

Before I got my guide dog I took some tumbles down the stairs. I'm still dealing with the back problems from that. When I applied for a guide dog, it took about eight or nine months to get through the process. My class was scheduled in June 2010. I graduated on July 17.

I am stubborn at times. I can be a bit overenthusiastic. I have a laundry list of accomplishments because that is what I do. I never felt "enough" growing up. I never felt *enough* of anything. Not pretty *enough*, not thin *enough*, not smart *enough*. So what did I do when nothing was enough? I needed control. I wanted more and more to fill the void that haunted me. This is where my compulsive behavior was rooted. I looked for a relationship in which I would continue to want more than the relationship was capable of delivering, because that was what was familiar to me. This was my "aha" moment—when I realized how deep the constant affirmation of worthlessness was.

I don't feel this way today, but I am still very hard on myself. It took many years to understand and accept myself. I am very frank about my life and my experiences.

I'm conflicted; in some ways I want to thank my parents because they were so morally and emotionally bankrupt that I was given the opportunity to develop an unbreakable will, along with some serious survival skills. I can't remember where I heard this but it makes so much sense: "You are only as sick as your secrets." When people refuse to speak out about the things that hold them hostage, inner peace and freedom will elude them. Courage is powerful because it is unexpected. Being courageous can bring you freedom; freedom can bring you knowledge; knowledge brings you choices.

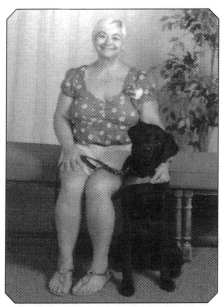

Me at Guide Dogs For The Blind learning new
freedom and bonding with my guide dog

My Guide Dog

9
Work, Work, and More Work

I left Boeing in 1997 to work for Group Health in Seattle. A network architect named Harold was in charge of the computer network administration and was tasked with finding a solution for monitoring network activity for the corporate computer system.

Harold chose a software package and hardware, never consulting with anyone in the program group. He tried to get it off the ground, but it never happened. The project was a huge problem. A couple of years later, since I had experience with the particular software he had purchased and had experience writing the complex scripts necessary make it work, I was given the opportunity to completely re-engineer the project.

Well, Harold did not take it well. There was a lot of anger and hostility. He would say things that were rude and disrespectful. He actually started pacing around the outside of my cubicle one morning, hitting the side wall of my cubicle with his fist. I wondered if I was going to end up on one of those newscasts when a coworker goes postal. Somehow I was not seeing this as an opportunity for me.

I let my managers know about Harold's behavior, and

they said they would have a talk with him. They told me to be patient and that he had a lot of stuff going on right then. As time went on, I held my boundaries. It was not fear that I would be hurt; it was more that I would have no witness when I whipped his ass. I worked so hard and put up with so much passive-aggressiveness with that project. I completely re-architected the entire project and brought it into full production, including documentation.

I personally trained all the support staff on all shifts on how to use the tools and run reports. I would arrive at work every day around five in the morning. Others started arriving between seven and seven thirty in the morning. Harold was coming in around six.

One early morning Harold came to my cube and asked to talk with me. My mind was racing, wondering what he could possibly want to talk to me about; my heart was pounding so loudly I thought he was actually going to hear it.

He said he was going through a divorce, and his son was the issue for him. He wanted custody, but his wife was fighting him. As I sat there listening, he went on to say that she was a thief and a liar and that he hated her. He punched my partition hard enough to knock off the papers stuck to the wall. He turned to me and said, "You remind me of her."

I sat there for a moment and thought, *Okay, I have no exit. He is in the entry of my cube. What now, hmmm?* I made up my mind to confront it. I stood up and said, "I have a lot to do, and I need to get back to work. I think you need to go."

Just then one of my coworkers came in. I think he heard my raised voice, because he came right over to my cube and asked me if I needed anything.

Harold said, "Oh, no, we were just chatting."

It was at that point I decided not to ever be alone at my desk. My coworker was in full agreement. I continued to keep the management up to date on Harold's behavior. Personally I think he should have been reassigned somewhere else.

One day the management informed me we needed to discuss how far I had brought the project. The meeting was scheduled for the next morning.

At five thirty the next morning Harold called my desk. There was no reason for him to be calling me. He asked how I was doing.

I said, "I'm fine."

He asked me what I was doing, and I told him I was working. He said, "I'm just watching the leaves blow around the yard." I stopped paying attention at this point. He rambled on about completely random stuff and then said he would see me at the meeting.

I said, "Okay." I thought that was weird.

Right before the meeting, he came to my desk to get me and tried to make small talk in the elevator on the way. At the meeting I brought everyone up to speed with the progress of the project since I had taken it over. Then my manager brought up the behavior that Harold had been displaying and how inappropriate it was. He looked at me, smiled, and said, "Oh, I called Becki this morning, and we worked everything out."

I was incredulous. *Was he kidding me?* That was not what happened. I told my management I thought he was capable of going off the deep end.

Eventually there were layoffs. They made cuts in many departments. Harold's position was eliminated, and he was laid off. I did not care. I was just happy he was gone.

A year or so later I ran into Harold at a user group for Hewlett-Packard. I was a web content administrator for the Seattle HP user group. I saw him in the hallway at the meeting, and he came up to me and said hello. I said hello. He just stood there staring at me. He said he was still unemployed. I was asking myself, *If you're unemployed, why are you here?* All I could hope was he must be there to network with people in hopes of finding work.

I stayed for a bit of the meeting because I was the web

content administrator, and when a break came, I excused myself. That was the last meeting I attended. Life is too short to put up with people like that. I should have just declined it.

When Don and I moved to Huntington Beach, California, from Bonney Lake, Washington, I got a job with a communications company as a systems programmer III. It was a killer job. I loved it.

10
If Life Could Be Like Movie Popcorn

I love movie popcorn. Maybe it's just me, but I get excited every time I walk into a movie theater and smell hot popcorn. I can steal away for two hours by myself eating my popcorn in the dark, just sitting there. I love it. I think I love it so much because I can lose myself in the darkness of the theater.

Funny story: I flew from Santa Ana to Sacramento to see my brother and his family. We went out to dinner and to a movie. We got our seats, and I thought to myself, *Oh— popcorn! I'll run and get some.*

I got up from my seat to get the popcorn and walked down three steps, turned to head down the hall to the door to the lobby, and slammed right into the wall. I cracked my glasses and got a cut above my eye. That sucked. I just stood there trying to get myself together, and then I went back to my seat. I laughed along with everyone else. I was more embarrassed than anything. That is before I had my cane and my dog.

My dog is everything to me. She is as critical to me as cars are to most people. She is the first thing I touch in the morning and the last thing I touch before bedtime. I know that I am still here today because of Dot. There have been so many times

I just wanted to give up and quit, but Dot keeps me going. I love her so much.

She loves to go to the movies too. I think she loves it so much because she tries to sneak pieces of popcorn in the dark. There are even times when my husband would drive up to the movie theater, and I would hop out and go in and buy some popcorn and come back out. The cashiers just laugh. They can't believe I went in just for popcorn. Yes, if life could be like movie popcorn, I would be in heaven.

I do have days where I'm so sad—I miss so many things. I miss my life when I was "someone." I miss wearing heels, driving, running, but the common thread throughout my life has always been do what needs to be done. I trust my intuition exclusively now. I just keep moving in a forward direction.

II
After the Quake

I don't know how I feel about Clint's murder, after all those years of justifying my anger at Clint for all the trauma he caused me.

When my brother read the fifty-eight-page police report to me, I did not know what to think. I sure didn't feel the way I thought I would feel. Was this internal justice? Or did Clint finally get what he deserved? This was a confusing resolution for me. I felt pain and compassion. I guess that is what needed to happen for me to move on.

The report stated that Clint had lung cancer and chronic obstructive pulmonary disease. I was sure he had mouthed off to someone in a bar who beat him or something like that. Somewhere deep down I wanted to hear that he deserved this, but he didn't. That's what I was picturing in my mind. I had every right to be angry at him and to feel as if he deserved what happened to him, but I felt sad at the way he died.

The report said that Clint and a woman he had been living with in Everett, Washington, had been drinking. Clint had been drinking most of the day. Personally, reading into the report, I think they were arguing and fighting, and she got the bigger knife.

Clint had multiple stab wounds. There were cuts and slashes on his face. He had a two-and-a-half-inch deep gash on his hand and a large cut over his eye that required stitches. They did not bother stitching up his hand. A plastic surgeon at the hospital looked at Clint's hand wounds and said they were not self-inflicted but were defensive wounds. When that passed my brother's lips, I felt that the internal balloon that was stuck in my chest for twenty years had just been punctured. The mental image of him being the victim, getting slashed to death with a large butcher knife, was pathetic and sad. The cause of death was homicide.

My brother looked at me and said, "Becki, this could have been you."

As we skimmed through the report until we got to the actual 911 call and dispatch notes. It was a domestic violence call: a man and a woman had been stabbed. Police and paramedics arrived and started working on Clint. They transported both injured people to the hospital. She had a knife wound on her neck, but it was not severe. Then we read through the police report page by page. I had never realized how much police have to document.

The woman's name was Kerri Marsha Henderson. When my brother read her name, I was creeped out; my name is Rebecca Henderson. When Kerri was questioned by the police, she claimed that Clint's wounds were self-inflicted. She said that they had been separated and that he had wanted to move back in with her. After she refused him, he stabbed himself. The report went on to say that she was on psych meds and had consumed three high-test beers. She also told the police that she had post-traumatic stress disorder but was not dangerous to anyone.

Kerri made more than one statement about what happened. She said she was not sure what happened because part of her problem was forgetfulness. In one account, Kerri related that she had just moved to a new apartment and was unpacking the knives, which is why the knives were out. Clint was there fixing some stuff when he told her that it was not fair that he couldn't move in with her. She said she told Clint that she wanted no part of it, and that Clint had picked up a knife and lunged at her.

Clint had a large knife wound on his neck that ran down his jaw just below the ear. Kerri said that when he stabbed himself in the neck, he fell to the floor. She then got on top of him and put her fingers in the gash to try to stop the bleeding while she opened the door with her foot and yelled for help.

Kerri made another statement that she had left to get Band-Aids and supplies for the wounds. The police photos of the scene show blood on the walls, blood in the bathroom sink, and a bloody T-shirt in the bathroom. Kerri said that she had to wash to go get supplies.

One picture shows Kerri Marsha sitting on a step with blood on her neck and a Band-Aid on her neck.

At the time of the report, Clint was in intensive care, hooked up to respirator. He was basically brain dead. He would overbreathe occasionally, but he never regained consciousness. He ended up dieing in the hospital, they took him off life support. The coroner's office had been trying to find a family member but had been unable to locate one.

At the time we obtained the report, about five years have passed and the police said that the case was currently in the prosecutor's office. There has been no arrest to date but in my opinion and it is just my opinion, Kerri murdered Clinton Brown.

I am glad to know what happened after all those years. I think sometimes about what must have been going through his mind as he was being hacked to death by a woman out of control. That mental image is very frightening.

I had never been able to find compassion for him, but at

that moment I was able to put myself in his shoes. I wanted to think he got what he deserved, but no one deserves that. I am glad I found out.

My older son Joshua told me once that it was sad, but Clint had made his own bed, basically. Daniel found his father's journals, and they both read them. They found that he had done everything that he was charged with. Joshua said, "Mom, he was like lord of the flies." Basically, Clint just lost his shit.

Joshua said he wrote him a letter while Clint was in prison and told him that he understood why he was in jail. Joshua said it was not all bad. There were sometimes when he was okay and fun, but that was not often. He wrote that he did learn some stuff from his dad. But he also wrote to him, "I don't know what your deal was, why you did what you did. I do not want a relationship with you, ever. If you come around my family, I will kill you." I feel bad for everything that has happened.

My son Daniel feels hurt because he does not have the memories of his dad that Joshua has. He has a hard time trying to remember Clint's face. I wish I had something I could give him. I always tried to do the right thing when it came to talking to the boys about their dad. I never talked bad about Clint to them.

12
Searching for Survivors

Since losing my vision, I have been thinking a lot about my life and what happened to all of us. It is very sad. We all had to survive in whatever way we could. I wanted to see my younger brother and my younger sister while I had some vision. It had been about twenty-three years since I had seen either of them. My younger brother Steve was in a band and was playing at a casino in San Diego, California. I went back and forth about whether I wanted to go. I thought, *If I go, will I recognize him, will he recognize me?* I took the risk.

My husband, Don, drove me down to the casino where Steve was playing. I walked with Don through the lobby. I was trying to scan quickly, but it was difficult because I only have a small slice of vision, and all the lights made it difficult. As I walked past the stage, I saw him. I hurried away.

Don said, "He just jumped off the stage and started looking for you."

I found a machine to stand by and started playing slots. Steve walked up to me and extended his hand and asked me, "Is your name Becki?"

I extended my hand and hesitantly said yes.

He asked me to stay after the show and talk. I said I did not know if I could, but I would try.

He started playing music and singing, and Don and I stayed to listen for a bit. Then I looked toward the stage and waved to him, and we left the casino. I spent the two-hour drive home talking about the meeting. *Did he look the same to me? Did I look the same to him? I wonder what his life is like.* A million questions were running through my mind.

After we got home, I just went about my life. I waited about a week or so, and then I went to his website and sent an e-mail. I got a response right away.

We exchanged information and decided to meet. We met at my home in Huntington Beach. We had a good visit. We spent several months taking flights back and forth.

I also got to see my sister. When I look at Daisy, I see a shell of what she once was. She was tortured by my mother. My mother died at home of a brain tumor. She was truly wicked to my sister right to the end. When my mother was dying, my sister took care of her.

Daisy has been in and out of mental hospitals for many years. My mother had told her more than once, "You are alone, you're going to die alone, no one wants you, and no one will."

When my mother finally died, my sister lost it. She had a psychotic break and had to be hospitalized. Eventually she got out, but she goes back and forth still today. It's very sad, and it breaks my heart for her. I love her, and I don't know if she feels that love. I can't take care of her.

So many lives have been ruined. My belief was always that if you lean, you will be let down, so don't lean. My situation today requires me to lean at times, and I have had to learn how to let myself lean.

I found my youngest brother at one of his
performances in San Diego Ca and my younger sister

My brother Shawn and family

13
A Hands-On Future

As my vision started to become more and more unstable, I wasted no time in trying to get something going, not knowing if I would lose all my vision or not.

I enrolled in massage school at the California College of Physical Arts in Huntington Beach after I visited several schools to see which one I felt could help me become successful in this field. I met Michelle Mangano, who is the dean of teachers and one of the owners. She made me feel comfortable and welcome. I also had the privilege of meeting Emily Cohen, a co-owner and finance manager. I started classes around July 2008.

About six months into school I fell and tore my right rotator cuff and had to have surgery on my shoulder. It was horribly painful at the time, but I have full use of my right shoulder now. I spent the next twelve months studying Holistic Health. Unfortunately, when I fell, I hurt three disks in my back, and my career in massage ultimately became impossible, so I had to think of another way to keep learning and growing.

I did take and pass the nationals. It was a very difficult exam, with a lot of traditional Chinese medicine questions. I was not worried. Because my school had prepared me so well, the test was a breeze.

After finishing my nationals I did a twelve-month teaching internship. I taught anatomy, pathology, aromatherapy, many massage techniques, and actions of muscles. I loved teaching. I made many friends, and I loved inspiring and encouraging the students. I miss teaching.

In August 2009 I was scheduled for eye surgery. A week after the eye surgery I took a trip to Sicily. Half of our family is from Sicily, and both my brother Peter and I wanted to visit there. I will treasure the memories of that trip with him for the rest of my life.

I was worried I would not be able to make the trip to Sicily, but my doctor just said to keep my head out of water. I had medications to put in my eye while I was traveling. A couple times while there I lost my vision to shadows; I was scared, but it came back. I found out later that because of optic atrophy and blood supply that vision instability could happen.

My husband stayed home and allowed me to have a beautiful time with my brother. Don graciously also wanted me to see Sicily while I still had some vision. That was a gift I treasure.

We had so much fun just wandering around. We went to Ustica Island in Sicily. It is about a thirty-minute ride on the ferry from the main island of Sicily. I found out from one of the local residents that in Sicily the visually or physically impaired residents are sent away from the coast to inland Italy during the busy season in August when all the Europeans arrive for their vacations. Ustica Island is where part of my family is from. I don't know why any of them left. It was absolutely beautiful. I did not want to leave. I could have stayed there for the rest of my days.

It was *hot,* like Africa hot, and I love hot. I love everything about the sun's energy. I love the waves the sun creates as it rises from the concrete. The smell of heat—that dry, summer smell—can completely change my mood. It often reminds me of a light at the end of a tunnel. Light, sun, warmth, brightness. All of these things seem to change my mood. I just found that contrast kind of interesting.

My brother and I took a rowboat out to visit Ustica's beautiful grottos, which are caverns along the coast. It was breathtaking—the water was emerald green and sky blue. The water was warm. It seemed pure. I remember every smell, every bump I hit with my cane. I go back there in my mind when I am feeling down because I was so happy there.

My brother and I had been sitting on a bench by the water when a local Italian guy came walking by and asked us if we wanted to go out in his boat. We looked at each other and said yes. After getting on the big rowboat I thought to myself, *What did we just do? We don't even know this guy. What if he takes us into one of these grottos and beats us over the head with his oars?*

I asked his name, and he smiled and said, "Paulo." I felt relieved after that, because his smile and behavior were so welcoming. He actually gave us quite a tour and history lesson of the island. We were so pleased, because it was just a fluke encounter we had while sitting on a bench. We will treasure that.

We also met a cab driver named Salvatore and hired him for the week to take us to all the cool places. It was fun: he was practicing his English, and we were practicing our Italian. He was such a nice man. His daughter was having a baby, and he was excited about being a grandpapa. He took us all over, shopping and dining and drinking. I hope to see Salvatore again some day.

Salvatore took us to Mondello Beach. It's a small town near Palermo, situated between two mountains. Salvatore took us up above the cliffs so we could take pictures of the beach. Then we went to the actual beach. Sand is kind of rough going—my cane sticks in the sand. I did not have my guide dog yet (Just one more reason to be thankful I have my girl Dot.)

The water was salty and just cool enough to refresh us. We lay in the sun for a while. We rented a pedal boat with a slide on the back. It was so cool. My brother swam and went down the slide. It was wonderful! It was really great to see my brother being playful.

As Salvatore was driving us back to the hotel, he pulled over, jumped out of the car, and ran over to a group of trees. He came back with some fruit. I can't remember if they were persimmons or what, but the fruit was delicious and sweet. I felt so okay there; I never felt at risk. I would go back in a minute.

I started attending the Braille Institute in October 2009. The Braille Institute is a great place to build your confidence and skills. I learned to crochet. I learned how to do mosaic tile. I can read Braille up to second grade. That is as far as I'm going. I was in several groups at the Braille Institute. I worked with the mobility instructor, who was very helpful.

I was in a water exercise class that was fun and challenging. The fitness instructor who taught classes at the Braille Institute had to stop volunteering because of work commitments. Since I am certified, I offered my services. I could not teach in fitness clubs anymore, and this was the biggest pleasure to get to bring my passion for exercise to all the people at the Braille Institute. I taught strength training and meditation.

Each week I would ask one of the seniors if they could go anywhere they wanted, where they would go. One lady said Hawaii. I went home and dug through my workout stuff and found a CD with Hawaiian music on it. My brother Steve had gotten me a special recorder and showed me how to use it. I set it up to take my students through a guided meditation to Hawaii. I described the clouds and the colors. I tried to involve as many senses as possible so it would seem more real. With my experience in aromatherapy, I could create orchid scents and flowery fragrances. I miss being there at Braille. I miss teaching meditation.

We left Huntington Beach in August 2011 and moved to Roseville, California.

We looked around for a house, but they were selling pretty fast. I ended up buying the house next door to my brother Steve. It is nice knowing that there is someone familiar right next door. My husband, Don, works remotely and travels occasionally, so having a brother next door is handy. We needed to be closer to other family because we weren't getting any younger. Our only options were Washington, Oregon, or Arizona. Well, Pacific Northwest—been there, done that, too cold.

Arizona is way too hot, so it made sense to be where we are. It is funny, because I live about seven miles from the house I lived in when I was twenty-four years old. Funny how things go full circle.

We had lived in a three-story townhouse in Huntington Beach for almost seven years. Three-story houses are not good for people who are visually impaired. After I hurt my shoulder, we started thinking that a house with stairs was not good, but we could not sell because we owed more than the house was now worth.

We talked with the bank that held our mortgage. We told them that I had become disabled, and I needed a single-story home. We found a house that was owned by the same bank that held my mortgage. It was already foreclosed on and was for sale. It was about the same value as our house. We asked if we could do a substitution of security; we would pay for any closing costs or fees or whatever was necessary. The woman I spoke with said the investors were not interested in doing this. I explained that my needs were medically related. I even sent them my confidential medical records and letters from my doctor.

Nope, they said; we could start short-sale papers, but that was it. So we continued in our Huntington Beach home for two more years. After a couple more ruptured discs and a radial contusion to my left wrist, the living situation became too much.

Thus the move to Roseville. I miss the beach, and I have an emotional connection to Orange County. There I experienced the best times of my life and the worst. I lost my vision there, and I made many friends in the blind community: my dearest friends Richard and Nadia, and all my good friends at the Braille Institute. We have settled in here in Roseville, and it feels like home for now.

Writing this book acted as a catharsis for my life that has come full circle. My passion is to help others on the journey to heal old wounds and find courage to face the new ones. I know there are many people who have gone through the same things as I have—and even worse. They may live in a constant state of emptiness. Nothing is going to fill it until we plug the hole.

In order for this book to be written I needed the time to do it. Looking back at my crazy life, I have had the opportunity to be grateful, helpful, useful, and successful. I am finally full.

Mondello Beach Palermo Sicily

Me and my older brother in Sicily
swimming in the Meditranian Sea

Self-portrait in Italy

Pictures of the Italy trip

Some of my drawings and painting

What kind of an individual am I?

Do I give back to others?

You give unconditionally and without an ulterior motive. In fact, you are one of the most generous people I've ever known.

Would you trust me investing 20,000 of your money?

Yes. Because of your thirst for knowledge, drive for success and cautious approach, I trust your judgment in making sound investments.

Would you want me on a team of yours?

Absolutely! Your ability to lead with diplomacy and follow with enthusiasm is an inspiration to your team.
Your teammates trust and value your opinion because they know you've done the research and can back up your position.

What kind of support do you think I would give to other team players

Your teammates can always count of you to be there, regardless of the situation. Your willingness to sacrifice for the sake of the team motivates others to do the same.

Email from my latest boss

Emily & Michelle

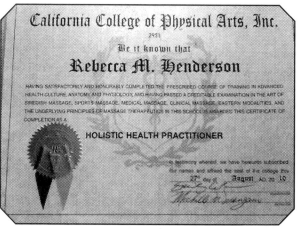

California College of Physical Arts, Inc.

2951

Be it known that

Rebecca M. Henderson

HAVING SATISFACTORILY AND HONORABLY COMPLETED THE PRESCRIBED COURSE OF TRAINING IN ADVANCED HEALTH CULTURE, ANATOMY AND PHYSIOLOGY, AND HAVING PASSED A CREDITABLE EXAMINATION IN THE ART OF SWEDISH MASSAGE, SPORTS MASSAGE, MEDICAL MASSAGE, CLINICAL MASSAGE, EASTERN MODALITIES, AND THE UNDERLYING PRINCIPLES OF MASSAGE THERAPEUTICS IN THIS SCHOOL IS AWARDED THIS CERTIFICATE OF COMPLETION AS A

HOLISTIC HEALTH PRACTITIONER

In testimony whereof, we have hereunto subscribed our names and affixed the seal of the college this

27th day of **August** A.D. 20 10

My H.H.P.

California College of Physical Arts

18562 Beach Blvd, Suite 11
Huntington Beach, CA 92648
NCBTMB Approved Provider 892445246

Certificate of Achievement

Rebecca M. Henderson
3009

Teaching Assistant

Continuing Education Hours: 36
Class Dates: 06/13/2010 - 08/29/2010

CALIFORNIA MASSAGE THERAPY COUNCIL

By authority of the State of California Code BnEP Section 4600,
the California Massage Therapy Council hereby awards to

Rebecca Marie Henderson

the designation of

Certified Massage Therapist

Let it be known by all that, having met the standards set forth by the California Massage Therapy Council and having demonstrated knowledge of applicable disciplines related to the practice of massage therapy, Rebecca Marie Henderson is recognized as a CMT in good standing, including all the rights and privileges pertaining thereto, as witnessed by the signature below.

Given at Sacramento, California, Wednesday, October 12, 2011.

Dixie Wall
Dixie Wall, Chairman of the Board
California Massage Therapy Council

CERTIFICATE # 28628
EXPIRES: 10/12/2013

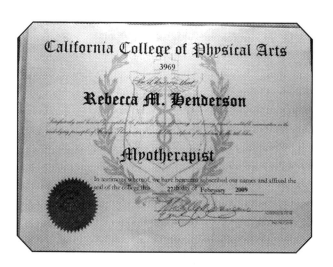

California College of Physical Arts

3969

For It Known that

Rebecca M. Henderson

Myotherapist

In testimony whereof, we have hereunto subscribed our names and affixed the seal of the college this 27th day of February 2009

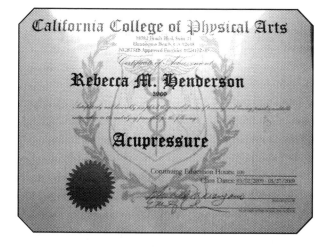

California College of Physical Arts

18982 Beach Blvd, Suite 33
Huntington Beach, CA 92648
NCBTMB Approved Provider #024352-00

Certificate of Achievement

Rebecca M. Henderson

3969

Acupressure

Continuing Education Hours: 100
Class Dates: 03/02/2009 - 03/27/2009

California College of Physical Arts

18582 Beach Blvd, Suite 11
Huntington Beach, CA 92648
NCBTMB Approved Provider #024152-00

Certificate of Achievement

Rebecca M. Henderson
3069

Satisfactorily and honorably completed the required course of instruction and training found to conduct examinations in the underlying principles of the following

Auriculotherapy

Continuing Education Hours: 25
Class Dates: 01/26/2009 - 01/30/2009

WRITTEN DIRECTOR/OR PROVIDER

California College of Physical Arts

18582 Beach Blvd, Suite 11
Huntington Beach, CA 92648
NCBTMB Approved Provider #024152-00

Certificate of Achievement

Rebecca M. Henderson
3069

Satisfactorily and honorably completed the required course of instruction and training found to conduct examinations in the underlying principles of the following

Reiki Master

Continuing Education Hours: 15
Class Dates: 09/24/2010 - 09/27/2010

WRITTEN DIRECTOR/OR PROVIDER

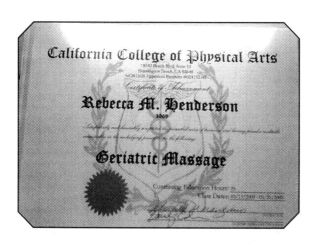

California College of Physical Arts
18302 Beach Blvd, Suite 11
Huntington Beach, CA 92648
NCBTMB Approved Provider #0024152-00

Certificate of Achievement

Rebecca M. Henderson
3069

Geriatric Massage

Continuing Education Hours: 28
Class Dates: 03/21/2009 - 03/21/2009

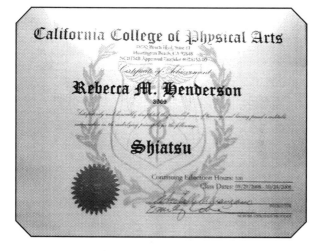

California College of Physical Arts
18302 Beach Blvd, Suite 11
Huntington Beach, CA 92648
NCBTMB Approved Provider #0024152-00

Certificate of Achievement

Rebecca M. Henderson
3069

Shiatsu

Continuing Education Hours: 100
Class Dates: 09/29/2008 - 10/24/2008

American Council on Exercise®

This certificate attests that

Rebecca Henderson

has met all the requirements of the American Council on Exercise in serving and employing fitness programs for individuals who have an approved physical limitation or special medical needs.

Certified
Personal Trainer

ACE CERTIFIED

National Personal Training Institute
Costa Mesa, California

This certifies that

Rebecca Henderson

Has successfully completed all the requirements in the Theory and Practice of Personal Training. This diploma is hereby awarded this 29th day of June 2006 and is recognized and approved by the California Department for Private Postsecondary and Vocational Education.

This designation title herein is that of **Personal Trainer**, and includes 100 hours of Theory & Practice of Personal Training, 150 hours in Basic Nutrition, 100 hours in Anatomy & Physiology, and 200 hours of Practical Application of Personal Training.

Certificate Number

Cathartic Release

There will always be a part of me that is sorrowful for the child in me that was traumatized. For the young woman who married a stranger of the heart and the mother who wanted safety for her children.

Feelings of deep distress caused by the losses and disappointment have overwhelmed me at times while writing this book. I am looking at "becki justbecki from a different perspective today. I felt anger, rage, pity, there were many, many emotions running through me like boiling blood running through my veins. Here is where the rubber meets the road, I could accept the darkness of depression and despair, live a quiet dark life of internal torment. I could choose to die right here. I can also choose to follow my heart. As I finish the last pages of this book, I think about the experiences I have had, mourned the losses of the experiences that I will never have. Digging deep down into your shit is a rough process that takes great courage. It is not just the writing it is the whole process of dredging up pain.

One of our friends in Seattle Washington had been building his dream home and I wanted to see this house that he always talked about. When I told our friend I wanted to see the his dream because I was loosing my vision. He said to pick a date and let him know when we could fly up from Huntington Beach, he would give us the cooks tour of his home. He added that he would also take me up in his airplane, not just a ride in the plane but I could fly his plane and have that memory forever. The thought of that was so exciting because I am an adrenaline junkie.

We set the date that would work for everyone and flew into Seattle. We met up with our friend and I did get the tour of his beautiful home but he never took me up in his airplane. I never experience flying an airplane. It was one of my greatest disappointments and I'm ok with that. I'm not ok with a declaration or assurance that one will do a particular thing and then not do it. It's called a broken promise. I expected someone who touts integrity and follow through to be more aware of there promises no matter how big or small. Thank god he is not in charge of the Make A Wish Foundation, LOL.

This book has fueled me. It has burned up negativity and made room for more positive ideas to satisfy me. I don't know how else to describe this process so I hope it makes sense.

So where do I go from here? I am in the process of creating a coaching and confidence building course. The "yea but" reason to fail, to not even try is unacceptable. We need to share our stories of triumph and courage in the face of adversity. I am creating a safe place to share knowledge and compassion and fears. My program is called COACH© 2012. This is an acronym for Courage Overcoming Abuse Changes Humanity. I am a walking example of a born COACH in every way. I have changed many lives in my travels. My life continues to change humanity everyday by being bold and opening my mouth. If we have courage we can change anything. I run into people everyday who are in some form of paralyzing pain. Abuse has given me the gift of keen intuition and enough energy and enthusiasm to help others. That is my goal and I rarely fall short of a goal.

I am a firm believer that if Life is a lemon, make lemonade dam it!

About the Author

Rebecca Henderson spent fifteen years in IT as an accomplished systems programmer in Seattle, Washington, and Irvine, California.

After losing most of her sight, her life changed. She became depressed for about ten minutes and then began to put her time to good use.

She started massage school, but injuries stemming from her vision loss prevented her from taking on a career as a masseuse, and she took a new direction in the physical healing arts and ultimately earned credentials as a holistic health practitioner from the California College of Physical Arts. She completed a teaching internship, delivering both core curriculum and continuing education classes.

She would volunteer at the Braille Institute in Orange County, California, where she developed tailored educational materials and facilitated peer support groups to help others deal with the loss of sight and related issues.

She has been a guest speaker and educator at numerous functions for the Braille Institute as well as the California College of Physical Arts.

Rebecca lives in Northern California with her husband, Don, and her guide dog Dot, where she tries to make it a rule to look at the shovel, not the pile.

Rebecca and Dot are available for motivational speaking and group facilitation.